YOUR KNOWLEDGE HAS VALUE

- We will publish your bachelor's and master's thesis, essays and papers

- Your own eBook and book - sold worldwide in all relevant shops

- Earn money with each sale

Upload your text at www.GRIN.com
and publish for free

Bibliographic information published by the German National Library:

The German National Library lists this publication in the National Bibliography; detailed bibliographic data are available on the Internet at http://dnb.dnb.de .

This book is copyright material and must not be copied, reproduced, transferred, distributed, leased, licensed or publicly performed or used in any way except as specifically permitted in writing by the publishers, as allowed under the terms and conditions under which it was purchased or as strictly permitted by applicable copyright law. Any unauthorized distribution or use of this text may be a direct infringement of the author s and publisher s rights and those responsible may be liable in law accordingly.

Imprint:

Copyright © 2019 GRIN Verlag
Print and binding: Books on Demand GmbH, Norderstedt Germany
ISBN: 9783668949355

This book at GRIN:

https://www.grin.com/document/468191

Miriam B.

The Influence of Modern Electronic Media on the Usage of the English Language

GRIN Verlag

GRIN - Your knowledge has value

Since its foundation in 1998, GRIN has specialized in publishing academic texts by students, college teachers and other academics as e-book and printed book. The website www.grin.com is an ideal platform for presenting term papers, final papers, scientific essays, dissertations and specialist books.

Visit us on the internet:

http://www.grin.com/

http://www.facebook.com/grincom

http://www.twitter.com/grin_com

Language and Electronic Media

How Development Influences Language Usage

Table of Content

1. Introduction 1
2. The Internet and Language Change 2
   2.1 The Function of Online Language 2
3. How Computer-Mediated Communication (CMC) Influences our Lives 3
   3.1 Asynchronous vs. Synchronous Communication Media 4
   3.2 Linguistic Aspects of Speech vs. Writing 6
4. Syntactic Properties of Computer-Mediated Language 7
5. Sample Analysis of a Blog 8
6. The Influential Power of the Internet 11
7. Conclusion 11

References

LANGUAGE AND ELECTRONIC MEDIA

1. Introduction

Electronic media, including the devices that were brought along, did become a changing power of society. While dealing with this changing power more closely, it becomes conspicuous that the Internet functions as a significant force. More precisely, it appears as an engine that keeps electronic media development going. Furthermore, the Internet stands for another massive influence concerning any human being on earth that is in favor of being connected to others: Language. To make it more specific there is talk of language change.

When the Internet's power is evaluated from a superficial perspective the thoughts that the Internet creates new words, makes prevailing words disappear, uses abbreviations instead and spreads the results on weblogs or other social media sites, comes to mind easily.

However, the Internet brought various changes. One of its obvious ones is the way people talk to each other due to modern technology; looking on a phone screen has replaced looking into other people's eyes. Besides, the society is not forced to leave their safe homes anymore because anything that might be needed is available on the Internet, ready to be clicked on. It seems like this medium has made life easier but what is also mandatory to take into consideration are all the negative side effects that electronic media brought along: The loss of punctuation and spelling skills due to texting and the need of including as much information as possible in as little text as possible or the standardization of using abbreviations.

Many linguists, such as David Crystal or Naomi Baron, already wrote on the influencing role of the Internet regarding the use of language and therefore function as the main sources of this paper. Furthermore, this paper is going to focus on the linguistic aspects of Internet language starting with language change, going over to the functional and syntactical features of Internet language, the distinction of speech and writing and a visualization of all these aspects within a sample analysis of a blog. The investigation of all these subareas is necessary to answer the following question: Is the Internet destroying language or does it mainly function as an innocent party in this case?

2. The Internet and Language Change

"The emergence of new technologies usually causes new words. In the case of computer and the Internet many existing words got new meanings, too, for example, the verbs 'to browse' or 'to surf'" (Greiffenstern 2010: 122).

The Internet has changed the way we communicate, the way we do organize our everyday life including the way we work out. Besides, all of these changes none might be as influential as language change. One can say that the Internet, obviously, created the Internet Language and therefore caused a new chapter of language change.

Language change can occur due to various triggers. "There are internal factor like language structure, and external factors like contact and borrowing" (Greiffenstern 2010: 81). In additions to those factors, Greiffenstern also mentions 'extra-linguistic factors'. "There are for example, sociopolitical and economic factors as well as social-psychological factors like identity and attitudes" (Greiffenstern 2010: 81). Moreover, it is important to understand that language change constantly surrounds members of society because from generation to generation changes occur in language and the usage of words. David Crystal (2006: 57) comments this with the following:

> In olden times (…) it would take several years before a new word would achieve a sufficiently high community profit to appear in print, be picked up by lexicographers, and come to be recorded in dictionaries. Today, a new word can achieve a global profile within hours. It seems likely that the Internet will speed up the process of language change.

It may do not need any discussion to agree that several neologisms only exist because the Internet made them. According to Crystal examples for those would be: "blog, blogging, and blogger" (Crystal 2006: 58).

2.1 The Function of Online Language

Before being able to talk about the online world and its communication possibilities, it is mandatory to characterize and tear down the aspects of its particular language, since this component is what shapes the online cosmos. In the beginning of her book *Always on: Language in an Online and Mobile World*, Naomi Baron (2010: 11) gives the following example that shows why the development of new words is a constant ongoing process that is highly influenced by technology:

> As technology has evolved, new devices have often been named (at least temporarily) by familiar words and concepts. The telephone was originally designed as a "harmonic telegraph." What today we call *movies* were first known as "talking pictures" or "talkies".

Nowadays technology is mainly used to be able to communicate even though one has to overcome a certain distance. The development that has become the most important one concerning the overcoming of this distance is the Internet. Saving time might count as the main aim of online communication. People do not want to wait until they come home to be able to call. It is more attractive to write message, preferably with abbreviations to safe even more time, to skip personal communication. The World Wide Web has revolutionized the possibilities of communication and made instant conversations even more attractive than the ones that occur fact-to-face.

In addition of categorizing the Internet as the modern communication-tool, Baron goes into more detail by discussing emailing: "[…] written messages could be transmitted only if there were a system for linking machines together" (Baron 2010: 12). Of course she refers to technologized communication and if one uses emails, another person has to use it too in order of staying economic. Nevertheless, this concept can easily be applied to 'speaker' and 'listener' concept according to the Speech Act theory because "language is used for getting things done" (Heylen 2009, website). If one participant is not aware of communication via technology and of the linguistic features within the online language world, a communication between those two would be presumably impossible because the participants would not 'link' with each other.

3. How Computer-Mediated Communication (CMC) Influences our Lives

The 20th century was a century of change, since it brought the Internet into domestic homes and therefore caused a revolution. The original theory of the purpose was abandoned very quickly and regarding to this Greiffenstern (2010: 1) has made the following statement:

> The Internet was originally set up as a shared information space for governments and academic institutions. In the first days of the Internet, it was not expected to develop into a means for people all over the world to communicate with each other.

The Internet is always seen as THE medium of a modern life and it "offers many opportunities for interpersonal communication.

Apart from emails there are chat rooms, listservs, newsgroups, MUDs, MOOs, instant messenger and blog" (Greiffenstern 2010: 2). Like these communication rooms show, the Internet brought the possibility for talking for away from the offline world. The topic and the ability of communicating with each other should never be underestimated, since this is what guides us our whole life, makes life easier and defines with whom we get along and whom we allow to step into our social circle.

According to this, Sandra Greiffenstern captions Internet communication as: "the most controversial one" (Greiffenstern 2010: 2). As she goes one she on the one hand says: "[…] online shopping, online banking and e-government have positive effects" (Greiffenstern 2010: 2), on the other hand she says: "when it comes to […] email, instant messages, chat rooms and text messages […] some see a negative influence on the use of language, fear a deterioration of language due to the language features" (Greiffenstern 2010: 2).

She does show the controversy in her statements as she opposes the positive and the negative effects that were brought along with the Internet. Besides of those already mentioned aspects there is still the fear of "[…] especially young people might no longer know correct spelling and grammar" (Greiffenstern 2010: 2). Obviously this would be an immense loss of language and the ability of using it. This statement is not at all made up out of thin air, since she mentions the fact that: "In New Zealand, pupils are now even allowed to use abbreviations and other language features from text messages and online communication in papers they write in school" (Greiffenstern 2010: 3).

3.1 Asynchronous vs. Synchronous Communication Media

It is not against expectation that the wide range of computer-mediated communication has many facets to offer. In terms of categorizing this communication type with the aim of understanding it better, one has the option to divide the spectrum into asynchronous and synchronous communication and investigate both contingencies. In addition to those two categories N. Baron (Baron 2010: 14) asks the following questions:

1. "Does the communication happen in real time (synchronous), or do senders ship off their messages for recipients to open at their convenience (asynchronous)?"
2. "Is the communication intended for a single person (one-to-one) or for a larger audience (one-to-many)?"

	Asynchronous	Synchronous
One-to-One	Email, texting on mobile phones	Instant messaging

| One-to-Many | Newsgroups, listservs, blogs, MySpace, Facebook, YouTube | MUDs (Multi User Dungeon Object Oriented)[1], MOOs, chat, Second Life |

According to Naomi S. Baron: Always on: Language in an Online and Mobile World (p. 14)

To make these categories more plausible, examples – according to N. Baron (Baron 2010: 14) – are given in the following to make distinguishing easier:

One-to-One: Asynchronous
EMAIL

This explanation leads us back to the first question from above: "Do senders ship off their messages for recipients to open at their convenience?" This question already draws the attention to the flexibility of emailing. It is barely common or possible that one gets an immediate response after sending an email. However, Baron clarifies its affiliation to asynchronism by saying: "Senders and recipients are free to broadcast messages as they see fit, either publicly or sub rosa" (Baron 2010: 16).

One-to-One: Synchronous
INSTANT MESSAGING

With instant messages it is the other way around, they belong to the category of synchrony. As the term "instant" already implies, those messages are only sent "(…) when I know you are online and there is good reason to anticipate a boomerang reply" (Baron 2010: 17).

One-to-Many: Asynchronous
BLOGS (= WEB LOGS)

Nowadays blogs are very common and popular. The way they work is very simple: One posts articles about topics of interest and others react by writing comments. This medium belongs to the category of asynchronism because, as well as with emails, comments are not answered immediately and this is also nothing that is usually expected.

---

[1] https://www.e-teaching.org/technik/kommunikation/muds

Blogs mostly work as "encouraging teenage girls to keep online diaries" (Baron 2010: 20).

One-to-Many: Synchronous

MUDs (Multi-User Dungeons/Dimensions) and MOOs (MUDs, Object Oriented) "MUDs are synchronous environments in which multiple players interact within a textually created imaginary setting. The first such online adventure game was created in the late 1970s [...]" (Baron 2010: 22). Although this type of communication does not fit into the 21st century it still was a medium were people could interact and immediately received responses.
According to Naomi S. Baron: Always on: Language in an Online and Mobile World (p. 15)

3.2 Linguistic Aspects of Speech vs. Writing

Compared to the offline world, the cosmos of the Internet and its language can be seen as a separated sphere with diverse rules that the majority follows. The confine characteristics of Internet Language may not seem completely visible at first but once spoken language is compared to the written one, the attention will immediately be brought to the significant differences of its linguistic features. It might be obvious that those two terms differ but to be able to understand the linguistic aspects properly, it is mandatory to be completely aware of the specific type differences between speech and writing.

David Crystal, who investigated *Internet Linguistics* in his book of the same name, researched exactly those differences and asked: "Is Internet Language closer to speech or to writing, or is it something entirely different" (Crystal 2006: 17)?

Crystal states the differences by saying that: "Speech is time bound, dynamic, and transient; it is part of an interaction in which both participants are usually present, and the speaker has a particular addressee (or several) addressees in mind" (Crystal 2006: 17). On the other hand, there is writing and Crystal says: "Writing is space bound, static, and permanent; it is the result of a situation in which the writer is usually distant from the reader, and often does not know who the reader is going to be" (Crystal 2006: 17).

With the help of linguistic accuracy, Crystal points out the "five main types, for written language: graphic features, orthographic features, grammatical features, lexical features, discourse features" (Crystal 2006: 8-9). However, the appearance of spoken language has to be considered as well because "[...] the use of speech will undoubtedly grow as technology develops [...]" (Crystal 2006: 9). This statement has been made in 2006 and to this present day, it can be confirm that Crystal had the right thoughts. WhatsApp voice messages are more attractive than ever and skype conversations with our smartphones have become a part of our daily lives, whether for a private purposes or as a part of a job interview. "In addition to the above mentioned five types, therefore, we need to recognize two more: phonetic features and phonological features" (Crystal 2006: 9).

Crystal made it visual that both parts, speech as well as writing, belong to the Internet and its language. "Internet Language is identical to neither speech nor writing, but selectively and adaptively displays properties of both. It is more than an aggregate of spoken and written features. It does things that neither of the other mediums does" (Crystal 2006: 21).

4. Syntactic Properties of Computer-Mediated Language

Besides Crystal, Naomi Baron also investigated those differences and opposed some features of instant messaging, e.g. concerning sentence characteristics:

SENTENCES CHARACTERISTICS	SPEECH	WRITING
Sentence length	Shorter units of expression	Longer units of expression
One-word sentences	Very common	Very few
Conjunctions	Frequent	Generally avoided
Structural complexity	Present tense	Varied (esp. past and future)

According to: Naomi S. Baron: Always on: Language in an Online and Mobile World (p. 47)

With the differentiation of the main aspects, Baron showed that the syntax of computer-mediated language does differ from the language that is used in institutions.

4.1 Abbreviations and Acronyms

BRB	be right back
CU	see you

FTF	face-toface
EIP	English for Internet purposes
CERN	Conseil Européen pour la Recherche Nucléaire
ROFL/ROTFL	rolling on (the) floor laughing

According to Sandra Greiffenstern: The Influence of Computers, the Internet and Computer-Mediated Communication on Everyday English (p. v)

Even though this table is just an excerpt of abbreviations and acronyms, it shows that the spelling of them do differ to the actual phrase like the example of 'see you' shows.

5. Sample Analysis of a Blog

"Those who blog, *bloggers*, carry out the activity of *blogging*, setting up a *blogsite*, with a unique web address in order to do so" (Crystal 2011: 238). Concerning media in the online world, blogs therefore form a new platform of communication and publication and allow persons with friends to become *bloggers* with subscribers. Blogs make it possible to share thoughts, tips and opinions on any topic imaginable. Since blogs only appear on the Internet their relation to Internet Language is obvious. With regard to their linguistic features, one blogs is going to be analyzed in the following. The aim is to authentically show the linguistic features of a blog in a wider sense.

The blog that is going to be discussed is by Pamela Reif and is called *aboutpam.com*. She is a young woman from Germany who became an *influencer* through social media. She became famous with fitness-based content, besides that she nowadays also shares her secrets concerning hair, make up and fashion with her subscribers. All in all, this blog primary counts as a lifestyle blog and is mainly addressed to a feminine target group what is assumed by the chosen topics and the design.

Example 1:

Hello guys ♡ better late than neveeeer. Finally managed to upload all my Instagram outfits that I wore in LA with the exact shopping links :) Hope you can now find everything you were looking for! But unfortunately I can't tell you where the swimsuits of the 2 photo shootings are from, 'cause the photographers brought them and I can't remember the brand :(

And I'm aaalmost done shooting all of the pictures for my book! So much work and I was literally shooting every day since I came to LA but it's so worth it!! There will be over 100 pictures that are exclusively for the book and that I've never posted before. Exciting, right?

Anyways, happy Wednesday everyone!! Aaaaand happy shopping!

According to: aboutpam.de by Pamela Reif

       This paragraph has been posted on *aboutpam.com* in the fashion chapter. When analyzing written language it is important to be aware that the author, obviously, only has words to describe any kind of emotion. According to that, bloggers become creative to transmit their feelings.

Hello guys ♡

- A heart follows the address. The blogger my tried to emphasize the all the readers are welcome and loved. Instead of the heart she could have used other adjectives to express her feelings but she chose to let a symbol express emotions. What be see here is an omission of lexemes. Another possibility is that the blogger wanted to replace the comma by the heart-symbol. This comes into consideration since there is no comma that separated the address from the rest of the sentence.

neveeeer.

- 'Never' is written with four 'e' at the end. This makes the assumption of excitement arise.

Finally managed to upload

- The personal pronoun 'I' is missing at the beginning of the sentence. This might be due to the fact that texts that are published on blogs should be rather short in order to keep the readers attention. Besides, this text could have been written on the go and in order to safe time the personal pronoun was dropped.

'cause

- According to Axel Bohmann "the lexeme *because* is in the process of expanding its syntactic variability" (Bohmann 2016: 149). In addition to that he mentions all the possible realizations of *because*, which are "cause, cos, coz, cus, cuz, and bc" (Bohmann 2016: 163). One of those variations was used also here as an abbreviation of the lexeme. This might be also due to the rather short online language.

Exciting, right?
- In addition to abbreviation, this is another type of it in which not just a word but a whole sentence has been abbreviated.

Blogs function as informative source in any kind of field. When someone wants to get tips and inspirations quickly, they visit blogs. Since the 21st century is a time where people also tend to be in a rush, time is very valuable and no one wants to spend half an hour reading for one fashion or lifestyle tip. Regarding to the societies' needs the Internet world offers platforms where information is easily accessible.

LATEST   FITNESS   BEAUTY   FASHION   TRAVEL   PERSONAL

The distribution of a blog into those chapters offers its reader an additional opportunity to be able to only read what he or she is interested in or specifically looking for. None of the subscribers has to go through topics that are uninteresting. In general, everything is made more visual. A table of content with page number would be completely inappropriate as a distribution because barely many people would want to spend the extra time to find the right page number just to read a short paragraph. Besides, the latest article always appears on the main page, in order to make it even easier for the reader to stay updated.

6. The Influential Power of the Internet

The Internet has a power that should not be underestimated. Naomi Baron (Baron 2010: 177) describes aspects of that power in the following statement:

> IM (along with email and texting) does tend to be an informal mode of communication. As such messages may be prepped with words like *cuz (because)* and *ya (you)* (…) In the same vein, abbreviated forms such as b/c, U or R accentuate the casual tone.

Besides abbreviations and acronyms, Baron mentions another aspect that the Internet has an influence on, namely "whether a clump of language should be one word, a hyphenated word or two words" (Baron 2010: 177). Baron shows that the Internet offers a wide range of various realizations of word forms and the most frequent one is the creation of compounds:

"The Internet may, in fact, nudge language toward more compounding […] Think of the spelling of URLs that we are constantly typing in when we do web searches. "Washington Boat Show" becomes "washingtonboatshow"" (Baron 2010: 178). Baron shows that the realization of words might not be based on rules only, moreover they seem to be the result of intuition and personal preferences since webpages differ in their preferably usage of compounds or hyphened words.

The last influence that N. Baron mentions regarding the Internet influence on language is "computer software that's too smart for our own good" (Baron 2010: 178). It is a fact that the Internet brought a portion of laziness besides development, too. In her example Baron discusses spell-check and "whether the word *capitalization* is spelling *capitalization* or *capitolization*" (Baron 2010: 178). She describes the laziness while she claims: "In the really old days, I would be driven to look up the word in the dictionary […]. In the not-so-old days, spell-check would tell me I had a problem, but wait for me to request the correct spelling […]" (Baron 2010: 178).

On the other hand, there are also influences on speech. Baron mentions neologisms such as '*moonlightening*' or '*asap*' and adds: "Occasionally, written abbreviations make their way into speech" (Baron 2010: 179).

7. Conclusion

Any time period provides own language patterns and rules and many changes have occurred over time because people, society and needs in communication changed. Regarding language change N. Baron mentions the following example: "Chaucer wrote the words "hath holpen" in his Prologue to the *Canterbury Tales*, where today we write "has helped." No grammar police come after us" (Baron 2010: 162). What Baron tries to state here is that as time changes, language needs to change too in order to stay economic.

It has been shown that the cosmos of the online world and therefore also the range of Internet Language is very wide. Like any other language, also this one did overcome a process of change that is still ongoing because 'language is a living thing' (Aitchison 1998: 15). The media, in any kind of way cannot be judged as the epicenter of language change because they are not the one instance that sets off an avalanche of language change. Furthermore Aitchison (1998: 18-19) says:

> The media are therefore linguistic mirrors: they reflect current language usage and extend it. Journalists are observant reporters who pick up early on new forms and spread them to a wider audience. They do not normally invent these forms, nor are they corrupting the language.

Aitchison makes the relevant point very clear: Humanity causes language change. Any human being is responsible for language change while they use the words that are spread by others and spread them even more. Therefore, the Internet does not destroy the English language; since it does not even cause language change itself. It just spreads what is already there. When it comes to the innocence of the Internet, it has to be said that the Internet can only be seen as innocent in terms of the creation of language change but not when it comes to the support and spread of new linguistic items and since the Internet is suppose to spread it completely fulfills it task.

In addition, it is also important to understand that language does not consist of one staying particular standard form. Those standard forms do change with language itself: "We talk about a variety of a language being the "standard", with the implication that any other version isn't good" (Baron 2010: 161).

> When technology is new (as in the case of the automobile), bewilderment - even fear – is a natural response. When a technology has become embedded in our everyday practices (as with email), a metaphor such as "email to your brain" is understood effortlessly. Baron (2010: 3)

Here, Baron emphasizes that not only time shapes technology but also technology shapes time. Change is often connoted to something negative but it is important to mention that change brings good results, too. If one would want to strive against language change by still using 'hath holpen' the consequence would be that this person would exclude him or herself because this is not an expression that fits into the 21st century anymore. Most importantly, it is the education system that shapes linguistic skills over years and the Internet, or any other medium, should therefore not have an opportunity to destroy what has been built up over several years, immediately. Even the permission of using abbreviations in school papers will not make proper writing skills disappear, since there is still the individual social environment with various generations that requires proper communication.

References

Aitchison, Jean (1998). The Media are Ruining English. In: Bauer, L. & Trudgill (Eds.). *Language Myths*. London: Penguin Group, 18-19.

Baron, Naomi, S. (2010). *Always On: Language in an Online and Mobile World*. Oxford: Oxford University Press.

Bohmann, Axel (2016). Language Change because Twitter? Factors Motivating Innovative Uses of Because across the English-Speaking Twittersphere. In: Squires, L. *English in Computer-Mediated Communication: Variation, Representation, and Change*. Berlin, New York: De Gruyter, 149.

Crystal, David (2006). *Language and the Internet*. United Kingdom: Cambridge University Press.

Crystal, David (2011). *Internet Linguistics: A Student Guide*. London, New York: Routledge.

Dąbrowska, Marta (2013). *Variation in Language: Faces of Facebook English*. Frankfurt am Main: Peter Lang.

Greiffenstern, Sandra (2010). *The Influence of Computers, the Internet and Computer-Mediated Communication on Everyday English*. Berlin: Logos Verlag.

Heylen, Dirk (2009). Understanding Speaker-Listener Interactions. Retrieved from https://core.ac.uk/download/pdf/11473605.pdf (date of access: 2018, December 12).

Reif, Pamela (2016, October 25). Shop my Instagram-LA. Retrieved from http://aboutpam.com/fashion/shop-my-instagram-la (date of access: 2018, December 16).

Squires, Lauren (2016). *English in Computer-Mediated Communication: Variation, Representation, and Change*. Berlin, New York: De Gruyter.

YOUR KNOWLEDGE HAS VALUE

- We will publish your bachelor's and master's thesis, essays and papers

- Your own eBook and book - sold worldwide in all relevant shops

- Earn money with each sale

Upload your text at www.GRIN.com
and publish for free